D1607106

JUN 20 2002

ANTONÍN DVOŘÁK

SLAVONIC DANCES, Op. 46,
in Full Score

Dover Publications, Inc., New York

This Dover edition, first published in 1987, is an unabridged re-publication of all the music from *Slovanské tance, op. 46, partitura* (Slavonic Dances, Op. 46, Score), originally published by Společnost Antonína Dvořáka, státní nakladatelství krásné literatury, hudby a umění (Antonín Dvořák Society, State Publishing House of Belles Lettres, Music and Art), as part of a complete works edition *(Souborné vydání díla)*, Prague, 1955. A new table of contents and list of instruments have been prepared for this edition. The illustration, the introduction by Otakar Šourek and the editorial notes by Jarmil Burghauser have been omitted.

Manufactured in the United States of America
Dover Publications, Inc., 31 East 2nd Street, Mineola, N.Y. 11501

Library of Congress Cataloging-in-Publication Data

Dvořák, Antonín, 1841–1904.
  [Slovanské tance, op. 46; arr.]
  Slavonic dances.

  Originally for piano, 4 hands; arr. for orchestra by the composer.
  Reprint. Originally published: Prague: Státní nakl. krásné literatury, hudby a umění, 1955.
  1. Orchestral music, Arranged—Scores. 2. Dance music—Czechoslovakia. I. Title.
M1060.D98 op. 46   1987   87-750088
ISBN 0-486-25394-5

CONTENTS

Slavonic Dances (First Series), Op. 46 (orchestration by the composer, 1878, of the four-hand piano series written earlier that year)

INSTRUMENTS

Piccolo

2 Flutes

2 Oboes

2 Clarinets (C, A, B♭)

2 Bassoons

4 Horns (F, E, D)

2 Trumpets (F, C, E, D)

3 Trombones

Timpani

Cymbals

Bass Drum

Triangle

Violins I, II

Violas

Cellos

Basses

l

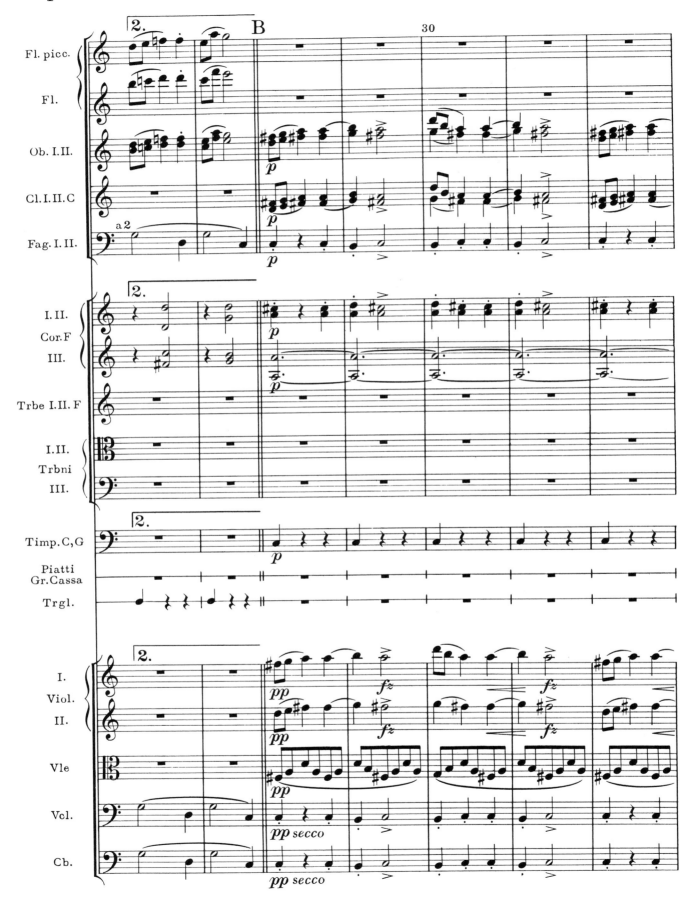

26

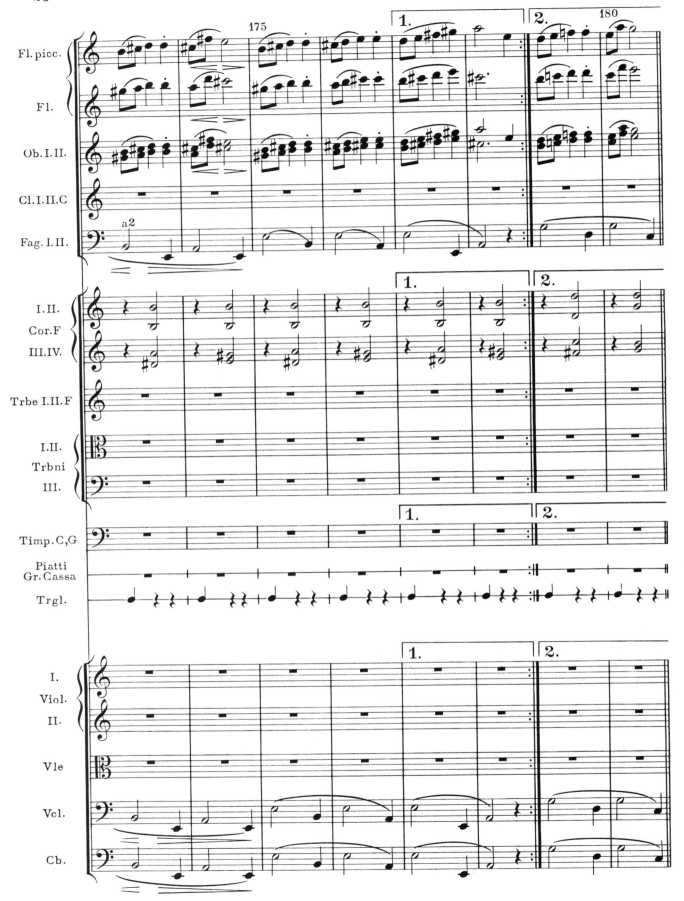

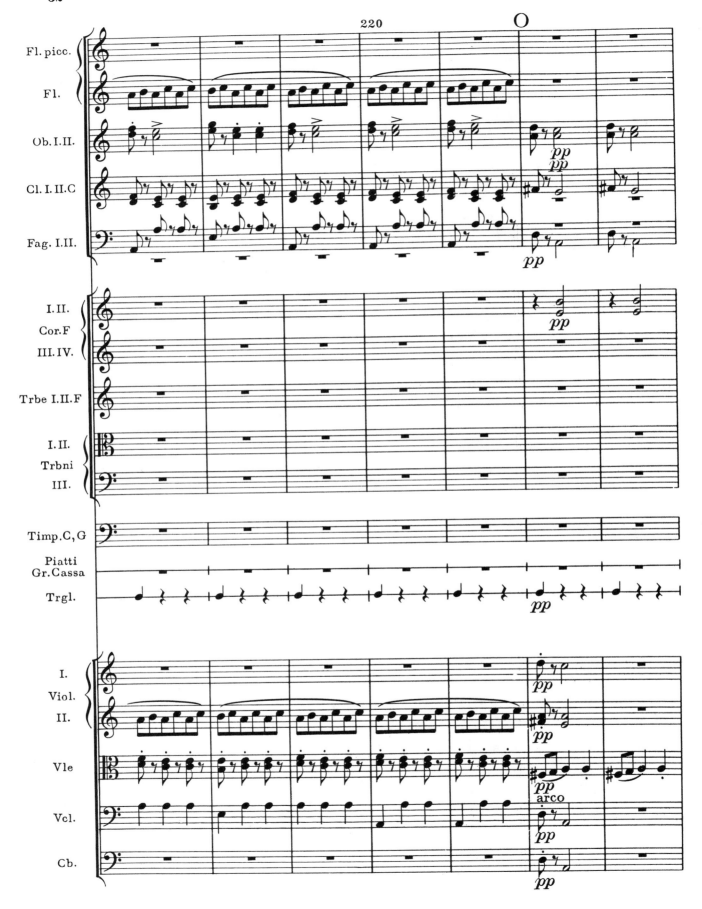

235

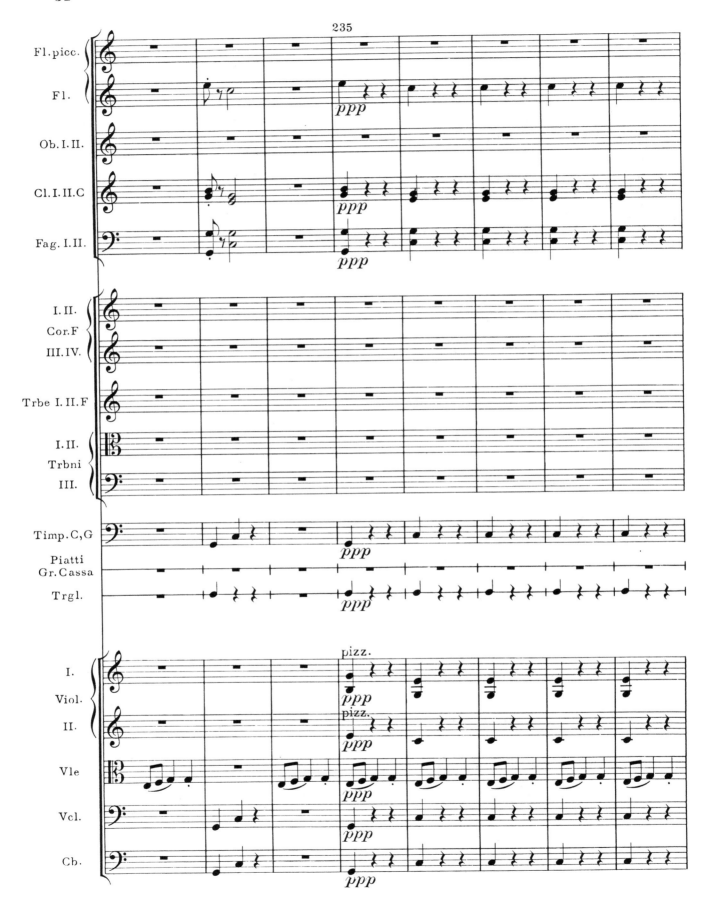

36

2

Allegretto scherzando

59

62

64

65

72

73

14. 7. 1878

3

*) II. volta: | — |

88

90

F

Più mosso

96

98

109

110

4

15

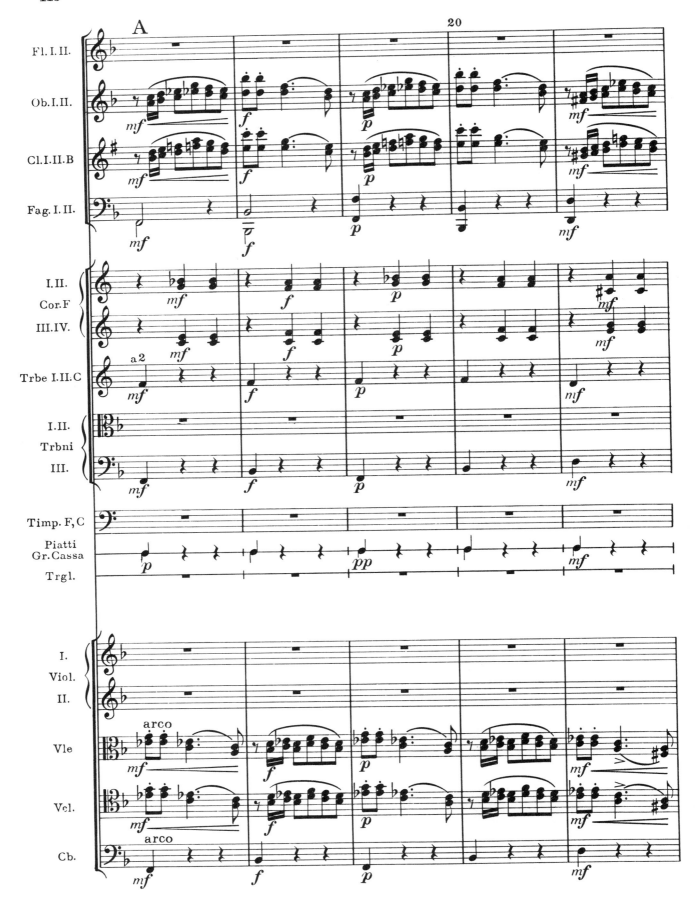

118

122

127

134

136

5

15

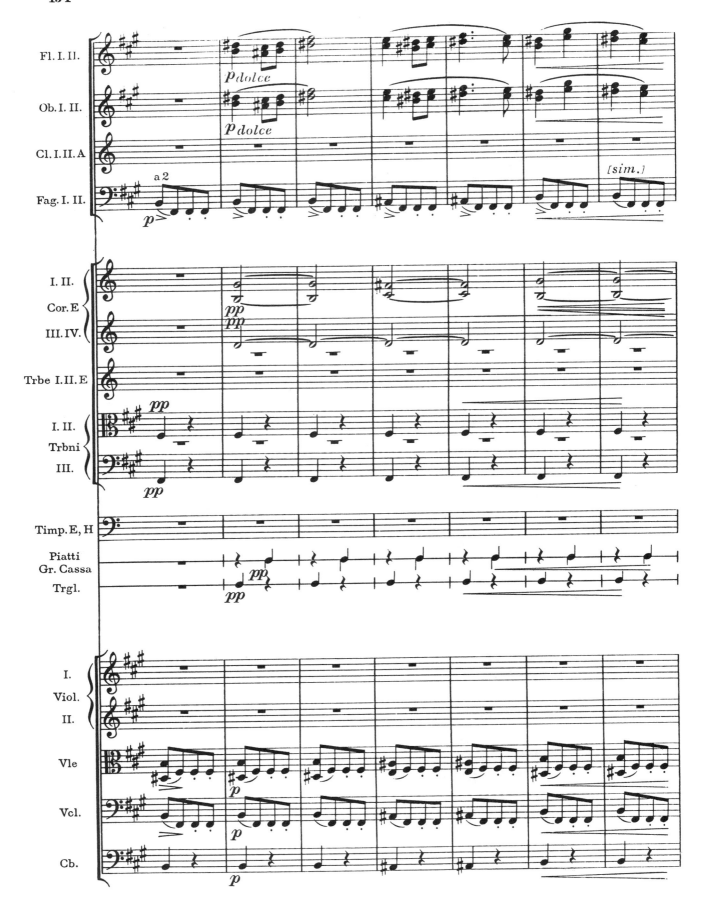

155

158

160

175

195

187

6

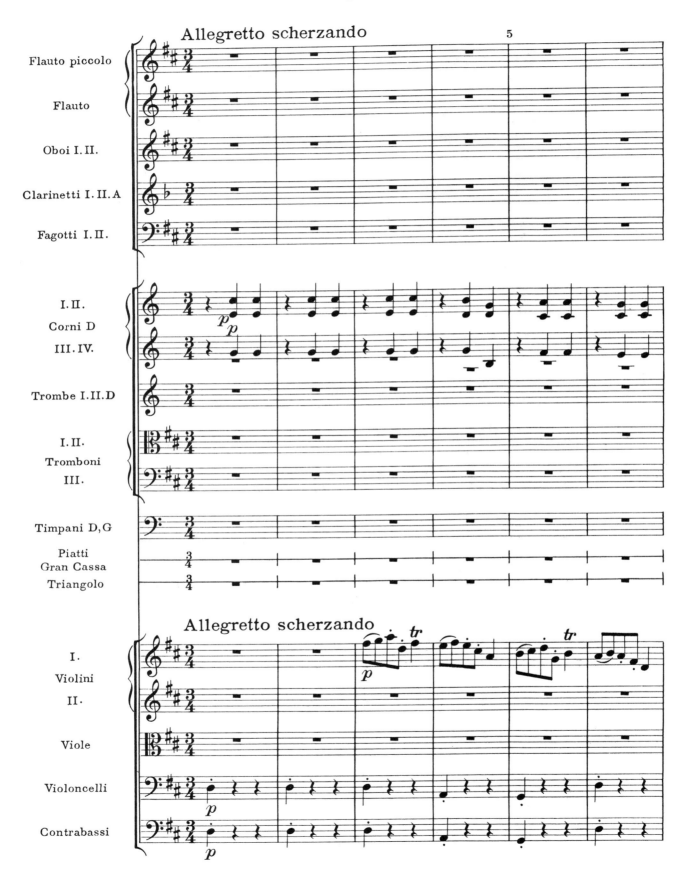

15

G

226

7

234

240

135

8

264

268

284

294